Confessions of a
Well-Kept Woman

Confessions of a

Well-Kept Woman

Satara P Ferguson

Order this book online at www.trafford.com
or email orders@trafford.com

Most Trafford titles are also available at major online book retailers.

Scripture quotations marked KJV are from the Holy Bible, King James Version (Authorized Version).
First published in 1611. Quoted from the KJV Classic Reference Bible, Copyright © 1983 Zondervan
Corporation.

Printed in the United States of America.

ISBN: 978-1-4269-2908-3 (sc)

Trafford rev. 12/30/2014

 www.trafford.com

North America & International
toll-free: 1 888 232 4444 (USA & Canada)
phone: 250 383 6864 ♦ fax: 812 355 4082

Foreword

Minister Satara P Ferguson is an anointed preacher, teacher and writer who have truly been blessed by God in all of her endeavors. Always displaying a high degree of integrity, responsibility, and ambition, Minister Ferguson is the epitome of how a virtuous woman should live and her second book, **Confessions of a Well-Kept Woman,** captured the core of her character and integrity. This poetic collection of writing calibrates the quintessence of who God is and the importance of having an intimate relationship with Him.

Listen intently as you read the pages of this book so that you may be able to hear the heartbeat of God and rediscover His purpose for your life.

Andrea Woodbine, Educator/Evangelist
Flat Shoals Elementary
Decatur, GA 30034

Foreword

by Evangelist Sandra A. (Milline) Parks

It is a thing of beauty to take something which typically has a negative connotation and make it positive. Is that not what God does in transforming us from sinner to saint? So it has been done in Minister Satara P. Ferguson's work titled <u>Confessions of a Well-Kept Woman</u>. When we think of a confession, it is usually admission to or declaration of guilt to some wrong doing. Ironically, the wrong doing here, if you will, is seeking, establishing, and nurturing a personal relationship with God. The spiritual maturity which manifests through the same also deserves mentioning. If pure, undefiled religion, no worship, can be achieved in this way, or could warrant criminal acknowledgement, then Minister Satara has confessed these deeds quite well. She has penned an intimate, heart-warming collection which can be used to stir the soul in daily devotions, inspirations, and meditation. The road to salvation and spiritual growth has been opened and paved. Basic, though profoundly important, Christian principles such as prayer, exercising faith, and personal relationship with the Lord pervade her writing and will surely permeate the reader's heart. Each essay in <u>Confessions of a Well-Kept Woman</u> leaves the reader with baited breath to see just what spiritual enrichment has unfolded and will yet unfold in the next reading. Saved and unsaved will surely be blessed by this book. It is an easy read, and personally, it brought peace.

Learning to be content in whatever state you are in can be a difficult lesson and journey. Minister Satara is exemplary in her Christian faith and walk, attesting that with God all things are possible. She is a true inspiration. Heed the lessons here and you too, male or female, can be well kept by the unchanging God. Thanks, Minister Satara P. Ferguson, for showing us a personal relationship with the Lord is one worth having and **is not and does not have to be** complicated.

Evangelist Sandra A. (Milline) Parks
Greater Fellowship Missionary Baptist Church
(Pastor – Johnny L. Beasley, Jr.)
Decatur, Georgia

Confessions of a Well-Kept Woman

TABLE OF CONTENTS

Reflections of a Well-Kept Woman

Glory to God in the Highest Praise! Hallelujah! I give praises to God who is the head of my life. It is an honor to be able to sing praises unto God because had it not been for the blood of my Savior, I would not be able to approach the Throne of Grace boldly and with confidence. My second inspiration book, **Confessions of a Well-Kept Woman**, came to me during the process of publishing my first book, **Handmade by God**. In a crazy sort of way, "Confessions...." is its sequel. I say this because once we realized that we were all created (handmade) by God and understand that He has forgiven our sins by Jesus' death, we will truly embrace confessing. We have already taken the first step in becoming a Christian (acknowledging that we came from God) by admitting that we are a sinner and that we cannot save ourselves from our sin. We repent (turning away from sin.) The next step is believing that Jesus is the Son of God and that God raised Him from the dead. And the last step is confession. We are confessing that Jesus Christ is our Lord and Savior. Once that confession has been made, guess what; that's just the beginning and the journey is life-long. No need to pack our bags and make any reservations, God will handle it every morning He wakes us up. No worries. No extra baggage. No cares.

Many of you are probably wondering how I came up with the title, **Confessions of a Well-Kept Woman.** A confession is an admission of misdeeds or faults. It also can be a written document acknowledging an offense and signed by the guilty party.

(We all have sinned and fallen short of the glory of God.) And as for Christians, confession is a public declaration of your faith in Christ. Remember in Mark 8:29-30, when Jesus asked His disciples who did the people say He was and His disciples replied, John the Baptist, Elisha or one of the other Old Testament's prophets? Jesus turned the table on them and asked them who they thought He was and Peter answered boldly, "Thou art the Christ." When Peter made this confession, he was confirming that Jesus was not just a wonderful teacher, a super rabbi, or the hero the nation of Israel expected Him to be, but that Jesus was the promised Savior. My confessions are an admission of my misdeeds. It is a written document acknowledging my offense against God and it is signed, not by me, but by the blood of Jesus. This is also my public declaration of my faith in Jesus Christ. As for the 'well-kept' part in the title, if you have a personal and intimate relationship with God, then it is self-explanatory. Be blessed. Be faithful and be consistent in your daily walk with God. Amen! Thank you for your continued support!!!! Love you all!!!

Satara P Ferguson, still chasing after God's Own Heart

Dedication

To God: the Creator of all things. Without You, there would be no me; therefore, this book is only possible because of You who can do the impossible.

I dedicate this book to my parents: Kenneth and Anne Ferguson for accepting me as I am. My siblings: Angel, Ken- t, and James 'Jones,' for always believing in me. My nieces: Annaliyah and Kai for being my biggest fans. My nephew Tairique: for being such a gentleman. My aunts: Eva Cherry, for always being the voice of reason, Gayle Ferguson, Mary Davis, Rachel Dunlap and Eleanor Ferguson who from the time I was born, urged me to strive above the challenges of life. To my great aunts- Martha Beasley and Gerlene Mitchell: for being the moving force in our family. To ALL of the uncles in my life: Franklin Ferguson, Sr., Prodis Dunlap, Curtis Beasley, Sr., and Mike Sadaj, thank you for being the strong godly men that you are. A special shout out to my family from Augusta, Georgia, the Royals/Lewis'/Blalocks for always coming to support me in all of my endeavors! You guys rock and I love each and every one of you from the bottom of my heart. You witnessed my initial sermon and attended my first book release party. May God bless you all richly and abundantly! Thank you!!!

Monique Doggett-Chase: You have been my best friend since forever. I love you and I want to thank you for allowing me to be a part of your life. Chasoray S. Newton, Sr. for opening my eyes to see just how strong I am! You have been consistent with me from the beginning and I thank God for placing you in my life. Reverend James and Sister Norma Curtis: You two are the epitome of godly living.

To all of the evangelists in my life: Andrea Clark, Sandra Parks, Lorraine Carroll, Margaret Nelson, Tory B Jackson, Andrea Woodbine, thank you for being beacons of light. To Jackie Blount, Betty Martin, Marilyn Thomas, Lillian Patterson, and Reverend Keith L. Reynolds, for being consistent in your godly walk.

To Pastor Johnny and Sister Patsy Beasley, Jr. and the entire Greater Fellowship Missionary Baptist Church family: I could not have made it this far without your love, support, and prayers. Thank you! Reverend Howard Marshall: for challenging the class to go beyond our limitations. Reverend Michael Parks and Deacon Murry Blount- for being prime examples of what fortified teaching looks like. To the Smith Brothers: Deacons Charlie and Ulysses, for their willingness to go the extra mile to do whatever it takes to get the job done. To Sisters: Margie Smith, Mary Ford, Joann Mapps, and Linda Williams for their unending strength in their service for others. I want to say thank you to the rest of the deacons and members of the mothers' board of GFMBC for all of your prayers, support, and kind words and for reminding me that anything is possible if you believe.

To Mother and Papa Green: for their generosity and to Mother Fleming for always rendering her service with smiles and hugs!!! To Pastor Timingun Smith: you are indeed a pillar of strength. Brother Leonard: the way you make that guitar sing is amazing; continue to allow God to use you. To Deacon Lee and June Williams: thank you for being a powerful, God-fearing and Bible teaching couple! To Ernest Ross and the Fit4You personal trainers for giving me the opportunity to say yes I can even when it seemed impossible. Thank you for your words of encouragement and the extra push that I needed to go for one more lap, one more lift and for one more push. And to rest of my supporters: family, friends, and loved ones: without you, where would I be?

In loving memory of: **Edith Bullock,** Your journey was commendable and your strength was unending. You kept your faith in the Lord and He did not fail. To **Deacon Fermen Fleming**: you stayed on the course and fought the good fight of faith. Your legacy lives on. To **Deacon T.K Carter:** Thank you for your strength and courage. You will be missed. **Uncle Lossie Hubbard**: your dreams for our future will live on . . .

Reverend Jimmy Thomas- you demonstrated that a few powerful words can go a looong way.

Mother Eva Taylor- you adopted me as you granddaughter and my son as your great grandson, your wisdom and tenacity for life will always live on in my heart.

Brother Mike Yarbrough- you had one of the greatest gifts and it wasn't just playing the guitar. It was loving people in spite of their shortcomings.

And to my cousin, Mary Blalock, you were the epitome of living for Christ despite setbacks and illnesses. Because of your strength, I am still standing and still strong.

And for my sons, HyKeem and Chasoray, Jr.:

HyKeem, you are constantly reminding me that because I am a woman of God, I am held accountable for the things I do as well as for things I don't do.

Chasoray, you have inspired mommy to keep pushing forward regardless of any obstacles. I love you both very much!

His Gift to Me

For the wages of sin is death; but the gift of God is eternal life through
Jesus Christ our Lord. Romans 6:23 KJV

An expert on pleasing His women,
His smile wrapped itself around my womanly curves,
surrounding me in euphoridic bliss.
As we took a walk through the park,
He turned to me and asked,
"What are the desires of you heart?"
Hesitating, I answered,
"To be with you through all of Eternity."
"Come," He said to me
showing me a world unlike any place on this Earth.
"Where are the homeless,
the destitute, the hungry
and disheveled likes of those
in the dark alleys of our
streets?"
Laughing, He answered,
"Woman, this is the place
of Eternal life, that only I can grant
to those who know and love Me.
For I can only give these things
to those who ask of it."
I took His Hand and held on to it
as if my life depended on it.
"Woman," He whispered
squeezing my hand
to comfort me.
"What are you so afraid of?"
I closed my eyes and thought
of those times when I sashayed into the night clubs

looking for love,
finding refuge in hurting loves ones,
and turning my back on the one true Grace
that could actually save me.
A patient Man, He waited until the first
star kissed the sky
and repeated the question.
Finally, I told Him.
We stopped by a river
and He dipped His Hand into it.
"The River of Life," He said.
One foot at a time,
He stepped into the water
and offered His Hand to me
to follow.
Again, He asked me,
"What are the desires of your heart?"
This time, I answered boldly,
"To be with you through all of Eternity."
He smiled and took me into His Arms
as if I was a newborn baby
and completely submerged me in the River.
He dried the tears from my eyes
and said,
"No more."
I stood
no longer hungry or thirsty,
no longer seeking refuge,
no longer alone,
but whole.

God's Endless Strength

Being confident of this very thing, that he which hath begun a good work in you will perform it until the day of Jesus Christ. Philippians 1:6 KJV

One morning my heart was so full that I felt as if I was about to bust. Have you ever felt that way about God regardless of your circumstances? I'm sure a lot of people are thinking to themselves, "How can this woman be upbeat all the time?" She must have more money than bills to concern herself with? Her parents must take up the load on helping her raise her son? How does she do it? Plus, it seems like she's involved in a lot of different things at church?

There's no secret key to God's limitless strength. It's because of Him I am able to smile in the morning. It's because of Him I am able to take the time to write emails every week. It's because of Him I am able to be a part of the Outreach Ministry, AVOP, MTM, Willing Workers, attend Bible study, teach Sunday school (of course, as a great assistant), and still have time for my family.

I think I have mentioned this once before in the minister's class at Greater Fellowship Missionary Baptist Church and how do we find the time to do the things we must do in our personal lives as well as help our fellow brethren in their time of need? When the teacher of the minister's class asked me how I find the time to take care of my son's needs, work full-time, and participate in all the activities at church and help my fellow brethren, I replied, 'I pray for first and prioritized my time.' Praying is communicating with God. It is during this time, when He renews my strength. He helps me to understand that I don't have to participate in every thing I have been asked to do and it's okay to say no sometimes. He wants me to ask for His direction because He may not want me to take on another project. In fact, He may have something else for me to do. He also wants me to be open and honest with Him. He already knows my weaknesses; He uses them to build up His kingdom.

In Philippians chapter one, the Apostle Paul is writing this letter to share his love and respect for the church in Philippi. He gave all the honor and glory to Christ Jesus. Have you ever asked yourself these questions: When others think about you, what comes to their minds? Are you remembered with joy by them? Do your acts of kindness lift up others? Once Apostle Paul converted to Christianity, he dedicated his life to serving Christ. Even in prison, he still lifted up his voice and eye to heaven. Though he longed to be with Jesus, he understood that as long as he was alive, he would be able to benefit others by helping them to grow and experience the joy of their faith.

Let's think about this, while he was in prison, he could have become depressed, discouraged, or disillusioned. Instead, he regarded his imprisonment as being appointed by God. While in chains, the gospel went forth. This gave the apostle more time to write encouraging letters that were later used in the New Testament. We all must take the chance now to faithfully and joyfully serve Him regardless of our job status or how much money is in the bank. I don't complain about my job, because I have one, and so many people do not. I don't complain about not owning my own home because there are so many people who do not have a place to lay their heads. I do not complain about how badly people have treated me or how they are constantly watching for me to fail because I serve a God who only sees the good in me and knows my fullest potential. He is the Master Craftsman who created me, a beautifully and fearfully made creature to magnify Him and to glorify Him in all I do. Don't you know that if He made me ... made us to do His Will, He will equip us to carry out the true meaning of our very lives? God will continue His work within us until Christ's return. God's work for us began when Jesus died on Calvary and His work within us began when we first believed. So continue to stand boldly for God. The work is plentiful but the laborers are few. Is He in you?

God's endless strength is best supplied when you are constantly praying to Him, studying His Word, and living out Christ every day. As Christians, we share equally in the transforming power of God's love. And love is the most important gift He has given us. Use it (love) abundantly. Be blessed for we are saved, sanctified, and highly favored!

Be Watchful

Watch ye, stand fast in the faith, quit you like men, be strong. 1 Corinthians 16:13 KJV

Something touched my spirit one morning on my way to work. I was thinking about the minister's class at Greater Fellowship Missionary Baptist Church and the homework assignment that was due the following Wednesday night. The assignment was: How are we to watch over one another in love? This comes from 1 Peter 1:22. Sounds simple, right? It is. My questions are: Are you keeping watch over your loved ones? What about the new converts? Are you praying for them? Things like this shouldn't be overlooked.

We often wonder why there is so much backbiting in church. Why can't we all just get along? Where are our tithes and offerings going? How is it that Sister Backwards get to be the president of the women's ministry when I've been here much longer? Is it true that Deacon Wayward and Sister Lottabody are having an affair? These are all questions that may invade our minds from time to time and you know what? When these questions do, we must immediately pray. We must ask God to keep our minds sober and focus on what's really important. One of the many things we should be focused on is how can we do more for our fellow brothers and sisters in Christ? For those who are on the sick and shut in list, we can send cards or letters, visit them at their convenience, and pray for their physical strength as well as their spiritual strength.

1 Corinthians 16:13 reads, *Watch ye, stand fast in the faith, quit you like men, be strong.* This verse is telling us to be on guard, to stand firm in the faith, to be courageous, to be strong and to do everything with love. You cannot talk about Sister Lottabody and Deacon Wayward having an affair especially if you do not know that for sure. If you have any questions about where your tithes and offerings going, you need to attend the annual church meetings. Paul is saying to us in 1 Corinthians 16:13 is that we must stay alert and on guard. We

cannot be safe one moment without it (being watchful). We must watch over something, watch against something, and we must watch for something. We must watch over our thoughts, our words, our actions; we must watch for something. We must watch against all sin, all appearance of sin, all temptations to sin, all occasions of sinning, and we must watch for all opportunities of doing well to others.

We must be watchful for anything and everything whether it affects us personally or not. Besides, if we are one body we are a band of baptized believers. If one of us is hurting, we should all be hurting. If one of us is crying then we should all be crying. We all need to step up to the plate and do a lot better than we are doing. Stop putting off making that phone call to Sister Right-all-the-Time just to check up on her and see how she is doing. Does it really matter if her personality and yours do not mesh well together? And stop getting on the phone to talk about what Sister I-Need-a-Perm-Because-That-Style-Went-Out-in-the-Fifties had on at church on Sunday. You, no, excuse me, we fail to understand that God does not like ugly and when you talk about someone or leave someone out of the loop on purpose because you two do not see eye to eye on a lot of things, we forfeit so many of our blessings. God alone doesn't always bless us, He sends people to do that very thing. And because we are too busy looking on the outside of the person; we may miss the blessings that God has in store for us.

It is un-Christ-like to have a clique within the body of Christ. People should not only hang out, call, or sit with people that they speak to on a regular basis or the people who willingly go along with your set of standards or ideas. Wake-up, please! Bible scholars, remember how Paul called out Peter for doing the same thing? STOP! Be strong in the Lord and in all His might. Remain faithful and be watchful.

God Does Not Change

For I am the Lord, I change not. Malachi 3:6

We need to start acting like we know that we know that we know who our Father is. We all must go about our daily affairs prayerfully and faithfully and consistently. Above everything else, we must remember that we serve a God who cannot fail, who does not change, and who is good **all** the time.

Once I realized just how good and merciful God is, I would wake up every morning with a prayer in my heart and His praises on my lips. As I get ready for work, I would pray some more. Once my son was up and getting ready for school, I will pray. As I prepare the morning coffee (for myself) and his choice of breakfast (cereal or oatmeal,) I am silently praying. Nothing too big, just telling God how much I love Him and how much I am looking forward to spending more time with Him later on during the day. I will kiss and hug my son goodbye before going off to work and I will say another prayer requesting the angels to watch over the bus drivers and the students on the way to their destinations. Do you see a pattern here? I am saying small prayers throughout the 'morning rush.' It is important to pray because you will never know what Satan has in store for you when you finally make it work (that is if you make it, because some people will not.) The Bible teaches us that we are to pray without ceasing. That does not mean that we are always in prayer throughout the day, but we are to have a prayerful mind and spirit. Amen?

What disturbs me is how we as Christians could go to church on Sundays and experience beautiful worship services, yet on any day through the week; the smallest thing can happen and we will lose sight of the bigger picture. Where is your faith? Why are we placing so much faith in the world's economy, when God's spiritual economy offers us so much more? Our world changes every day. People change every day. Our jobs are here one day and are gone the next. Yet, we choose to continue to put more faith in the temporal things of this world as opposed to the One True Person who does not change. That person is God. Remember when the disciples were on a boat and they noticed a figure out on the sea and that figure was Jesus? Do you remember when Peter boldly stepped out in faith to meet Jesus? Ask yourself: Do I tend to step out boldly in faith toward Jesus; or do I allow the turbulent seas of life to stop me? Peter stepped out in faith but his faith faltered when he took his eyes off Jesus. Don't allow turbulent seas to distract you from Jesus. Instead, pray for immovable faith.

The bottom line is this: when you have a serious relationship with God and by this, I mean you pray to Him, not just asking for blessings or healings or things concerning the temporal world but you praise Him. You praise Him through the good and the bad times in your life. You lift Him up even when you are tired and need rest. You lift Him up whether your bills are paid or not. You lift Him up whether or not your spouse or loved one is treating you right. You lift Him up when one door closes, because in your heart, you know that God will open another door that no man can close. Amen? Moreover, we need to stop playing church and acting all 'religious' and get on board with our Creator. After all, if it wasn't for Him, none of us would be here.

Grace Under Pressure

But without faith it is impossible to please him: for he that cometh to God must believe that he is, and that is a rewarder of them diligently seek him.
Hebrews 11:6

I cannot help but to think of the Apostle Paul concerning this subject matter: *Grace under Pressure*. Many of us are facing financial difficulties, health issues, relationship issues, and spiritual deflation. It is sad but true. We can spend most of our time at church, but as far as being saved and sanctified, we are not. We have not grown an inch of spirituality since we first sat in the pew. And honestly, it is not the pastor's fault. We chose not to open our Bibles throughout the week. We chose not to spend any time with our heavenly Father in communion. We chose not to pray and ask for forgiveness. We chose not to live out Christ every day. We chose to remain selfish, self-righteous, and uncooperative with the Holy Spirit.

Grace under pressure is how we react when our backs are up against the storms of life. Remember in 2008 when there was a gas scarcity and people acted like the world were coming to an end? People would spend hours in line overnight just to get a few dollars of gas in their tanks. That was crazy, right? I remembered looking at the news thinking, 'if only those people would put their trust in God.' Doesn't He make a way out of no way? Now honestly, if I had told you that gas was going to become readily available and the prices would drop significantly, you all would have looked at me like I was crazy right? Tell the truth and shame the devil.

Anyway, it's time like those where you faith comes into play; into action. That's why the Bible stresses why we shouldn't put so much faith in man, but in God. He sees all and knows all. Man cannot even predict the weather let alone when and where every thing is going to take place. Paul didn't know when he was going to die or even how he was going to die. But he knew God and he knew of the promises that God had made to him. He wasn't afraid of death because he knew he had stayed on the course and fought the good fight.

Pray to remove those mountains out of your life or pray for the strength of endurance to move up or around those mountains. Everything in life wasn't meant to be easy. If things were easy, would you appreciate them as much? Plus, if God is in you, truly in you, you would definitely enjoy any time spent with Him regardless of what your circumstances may be. May the grace of God be with you.

Having a Powerful Prayer Life

Pray without ceasing. 1 Thessalonians 5:17 KJV

To have a powerful prayer life, one must have a deep, intimate relationship with God. We Christians tend to have a vending machine mentality when it comes to serving our God. Whatever we want or feel we should have, we will make our requests known before God. However, as the loving parent that He is, God gives us what is genuinely good for us. God wants us to be saved from ourselves, from destruction, and from isolation. God wants us live in the light of truth, fulfilling our creative purpose. For when we pray, we will be changed.

We cannot get to know God without constant prayer. We cannot build a deep relationship without it. God cannot shape us if we are not opened to being shaped. Psalm 145:17-20 reveals three promises about prayer. 1) God promises to draw near to all who call upon Him. 2) God promises to fulfill the desires of those who fear Him. 3) God promises to watch over all who love Him. As I shared with the teenage girls' Sunday school class, God wants us to have a 'best friend' relationship with Him. He wants us to come to Him pouring out our deepest fears or our biggest dreams.

John 15:7, according to my Life Application Study Bible NLT states, '*But if you remain in me and my words remain in you, you may ask for anything you want, and it will be granted.*' Remaining in Christ means that you believe that He is God's Son, you have received Him as your Lord and Savior, you do what God says do. You will continue to believe the Good News and love one another. In other words, once you have established a personal relationship with God, He will talk to you just like you talk to Him. And if He's talking to you, then His Words will abide in you.

Sometimes, to keep from having a dull prayer life, I will keep the following things in mind as I pray. I will keep my prayers big. I pray with a sense of knowing just who God is and why I am praying. I will keep my prayers real: I pray with an honest understanding of myself. I know that I am not perfect and I don't always do what God wants me to do. And it's better to stay honest and lay out all the cards before Him. I keep my prayers personal: the main focus of my prayer is to know God and what would He like for me to do for Him that day. I will keep my prayers simple: the amount of words is not what define prayers but the matter of my heart which is expressing itself. I will also keep praying: the more I pray the better that I will get at it. I try to focus on a different method, a different word, a different place, and a different style.

I love you all and I pray that your prayer life will strengthen not only your personal relationship with God, but with His people as well. I honestly believe that if you are truly living for God, He will answer your requests. The results of your prayers may not come in the form you want, but God gives us His best every day and because He knows all and sees all; what He gives us is far better than we could ever ask for or dare to dream.

Have a blessed mentality because you are blessed! Think of others, do something nice for people (whether you like/know them or not.) The rewards are heavenly!

I Can Do All Things Through Christ Which Strengthens Me

I can do all things through Christ which strengtheneth me.
Philippians 4:13 KJV

I sent out a text message one morning asking, "What would you attempt to do if you knew you could not fail?" One Sunday while I was on my way to church, I received a phone call asking me to teach Sunday school for the adults. I've taught Sunday school for the Prek-2nd grade class, the Young Adults and now I am teaching the Teenage Girls. However, the adult class is where most of our deacons and ministers sit in on as well as the pastor. I said to myself, "Are you for real? Do you really expect me to go into a room where men ad women who have been walking with God as long as I have been alive and teach Sunday School?" Initially, I told the caller no because I was too busy looking at my limitations. But God ever so gently nudged me, reminding me that His power in me is limitless. Then I said yes.

Yes! Yes! Yes! This is what we should be telling God every time He asks us to do something. And the mistake I almost made was walking away from something before I even tried it. We need to stop second guessing ourselves and remember who our God is. He will never send us anywhere ill prepared or ill equipped, but we also must keep in mind that we are responsible for doing our part too. We must study to show ourselves approved unto God. Don't take for granted that the Sunday school teacher or even the minister who delivers the message will feed us what we need for the week. We must feed ourselves and if we don't know how to feed ourselves then we need to ask our pastor or a minister or anyone we know who has an intimate relationship with God.

Ask yourself what you would attempt to do if you knew you could not fail and then do it. With that question in mind, always remember where your Source comes from. We can do all things through Christ which strengthens us....Amen.

Jesus' Yoke

Come unto me, all ye that labor and are heavy laden, and I will give you rest. Take my yoke upon you, and learn of me: for I am meek and lowly in heart: and ye shall find rest unto your souls. For my yoke is easy, and my burden is light. Matthew 11:28-30 KJV

In Matthew 11:28-30, Jesus told those who were burdened and heavy laden to come to Him and rest. He also told them to take His yoke and learn from Him. When I first encountered these Scriptures, I thought to myself about the yoke and why Jesus would use that particular word. A yoke is a wooden beam which is used between a pair of oxen to allow them to pull a load. It literally means a band, or something that binds. When Jesus extended this invitation to those to come to Him, He did not add any qualifications. If you want to become a Christian, go to Him with all of your problems, all your troubles, your concerns and cares. Don't try to clean yourself up or make yourself better, just come to Him as you are. And when you take Jesus' yoke upon you that means you are submitting to Him and to His leadership. To do that is to live as a Christian is intended to live.

After my initial sermon, a visiting reverend told me to take Jesus' yoke because it is easy. Wow! How powerful were those words!!! Jesus' yoke is easy because He never prohibits anything, never imposes any restraints except for your own good. Unlike the oxen, Christians have a free will or a choice to serve. It's like an invitation. You could either accept it or decline it. Once you accept Jesus Christ as your Lord and Savior, He will give you rest. Not saying that you would never have to work another day in your life, you must work and work hard, but He will lighten your load. He'll carry the heavier stuff leaving you with all the lighter stuff to carry. Amen?

This blessing is this simple. All one must do is accept Jesus' yoke. Instead of walking around at your job allowing the devil to get back at you for turning your back on him, shrug that devil off and hand him over to God to deal with. Just be still and let it all go to God to handle. Try this: close your eyes and imagine Jesus handling all of your troubles, problems and ailments and putting those things in a box labeled 'Nothing is Impossible.' Once you have opened your eyes, you will feel nothing but the abundance of His peace and His love, and to me, that is priceless and worth the effort. Be blessed and stress-free.

Let God Be God

"And God said unto Moses, I AM THAT I AM," Exodus 3:14 KJV

God is awesome all by Himself. He is Creative (He made something out of nothing). He is Majestic (He is a true Royal King!) He is Honest and Just. (He is who He says He is and He will do what He says He will do.) He is a Provider. (He takes care of and handles all of our needs.) He is a Healer. (Better than any doctor I know.) He is a Way maker. (Didn't think those mountains were coming down, but my God made it possible.) He is a Strong Arm. (My enemies bowed before me.) He's the Bridge-over-Troubled-Waters. (How many times have my back been up against the wall and my God fought my battles and won?) He's the Lily in the Valley. (Ever been in the valley of the shadow of the death? So have I and God has always been there with me...walking beside me. And every time I felt like giving up, He would renew my strength.)

Whenever you feel sad, lonely, or stressed-out, draw strength from God and let Him be God. He is always there waiting for us to lean and depend on Him. He didn't create us so that we would go through life failing at everything and living miserably. He created us so that we would depend on Him for all of our needs. That's why it is a sin to worry. Don't just go to a cliff and leap off, be still and know that He is God. When He is ready for you to leap, He'll give you wings and just like eagles, you will soar!!!!

Be blessed! Be nicer to people. Smile more, laugh harder and cry sometimes. Jesus wept. Oh yeah, for you penny-pinchers, let that go too. God does love a cheerful giver!! You came into the world with nothing and you will leave with nothing. Peace!

More Than That

"Nay, in all these things we are more than conquerors through him that loved us." Romans 8:37 KJV

In the book of Philippians 3:17-21;4:2-9, the Apostle Paul's focus for the Philippians church was to have joy in Jesus regardless of their circumstances. They should rejoice in every circumstance whether they are sick, hungry, cold, homeless, or in pain. There are two reasons why we should all rejoice in spite of our circumstances. The first one is: we have so much to look forward to with a permanent home in heaven. The second one is: we should also rejoice because of our testimony to others. The Apostle Paul was in prison at the time he had written this letter. He could have become depressed, discouraged, or disillusioned. Instead, he regarded his imprisonment as being appointed by God. Though he was imprisoned, the gospel was brought to the center of Rome. This gave the apostle a lot of time to write letters to the different churches in which later became a part of the New Testament.

Through the life of Paul, I have learned that regardless of where we are in our lives, regardless of our social status, finances, jobs, or family status, God has us in place to faithfully and joyfully serve Him. I am going to share with you what I shared with both the Sunday school class and children's church. To have joy in God comes from not only reading the Word of God; but from studying the Word. The Word is a seed. It does not come to life inside of you until you allow the Word to take root in the depth of your soul. You must take the Word and apply it to your daily life and allow it to manifest inside of you. It will grow and when it does, you must then share it with others.

One of several things I took from this particular letter written to the Philippians church was that our inner attitudes do not have to reflect our outward circumstances. Paul was so full of joy because He knew that no matter what happened to him, he knew that Christ was with him. When Paul told the church to be careful for nothing, he meant for them not to be bogged down with problems. He wanted them to take their problems to God in prayer. Our thoughts affect everything we do. If we check our thoughts by God's list, we would avoid sinful actions. We cannot help some thoughts from coming into our minds, but we do not have to keep them there.

We must understand that our real home is not in this world. Do not build up on earthly treasures because eventually they will fade away. We should always focus on God and the peace His gives us. This gift of peace that God gives us comes from prayer and supplication with thanksgiving. He does not want us to be hurting inside and He will give us peace in the middle of a storm. This does not mean we will not have trials and tribulations but He did promise that He will be with us and give us the strength to endure.

Our Mission Field

"Go ye therefore, and teach all nations, baptizing them in the name of the Father, and of the Son, and of the Holy Ghost: Teaching them to observe all things whatsoever I have commanded you: and, lo, I am with you always, even unto the end of the world. Amen." Matthew 28:19-20 KJV

Too many 'Christians' are bench warmers or pew warmers or pew potatoes....however it is worded, it still means the same thing: There are too many Christians taking up space. Jesus told His disciples before His ascension to 'go and make disciples of all nations, baptizing them in the name of the Father and of the Son and of the Holy Spirit, and teaching them to obey everything I have commanded.' (Matt 28:19-20, NIV) Jesus gave the disciples a purpose, to share the Good News about Jesus with others.

We are all called to follow in the disciples' footsteps and to complete the mission the disciples were given nearly 2000 years ago. We are to share the Good News about Jesus with those we encounter in our world, to make disciples of those who accept Jesus, and to teach believers to be obedient. Let me ask you two questions: How are you doing as a witness for Christ and how can you make your life a stronger testimony? Meditate and pray on those questions throughout the weeks ahead. I want you to do that because so many times we're so caught up with our own concerns that we fail to discern who in our world needs to hear about Jesus. We all have a mission field, a place where God has planted us so that He can reach others through us.

Pay attention to the people God brings you in contact with during the upcoming weeks and what opportunities these present for sharing your faith. Make an effort to share the Gospel with at least one non-believer every week. Also, I want you to keep in mind that when we actively witness for the Lord, we demonstrate the impact that our faith is having in our lives. When our outward life reflects true faith, others are drawn to us and then to Christ.

Sharing His Glory as Well as Sharing His Suffering

"Neither is there any creature that is not manifest in his sight: but all things are naked and opened unto the eyes of him with whom we have to do." Hebrews 4:13 KJV

I send inspirational texts Monday through Friday and occasionally on the weekends; these are short insights to give people a boost for the week or for the day. That's my calling. It's a 'burden' that I bare. I had the opportunity to talk to a good mentor/friend/ mother-figure /'shero' about everything under the sun (or so it seems). One of the things she mentioned was her 'title' evangelist. I immediately thought of my own 'title' minister because that word means servant. Being a servant of God is who I am. It fits me perfectly. That's what God destined me to be. You can go to Romans 8:28-30 for a more in depth understanding. God works in everything for our good. Even when bad things happened, God will take those circumstances and turn them around for our good. God's ultimate goal for us is to make us more like Christ. As we become more and more like Him, we discover our true selves, the persons we were created to be. How can we become more like Christ? Why is it important for us to share His suffering as well as His glory? The first answer is simple: to be more Christ like we must read and heed His Word, study His life on earth through the Gospels, spend time in prayer, be filled with His Spirit, and do His work in the world.

The second question isn't so simple. Why is it important for us to share Jesus' suffering as well as His glory? When Jesus was in the garden, He prayed, "not my will, but thine." He had no tears for His own grief, but sweat drops of blood for us. He took our sins and sorrows and He made them His own. As the Son of Man, He did not come to have people serve Him; rather He served them. He did not demand a palace; rather, He chose a life in which He had no place to lay His head. He sought neither the praise and approval of men nor a life of power and prestige; rather He chose to be meek and lowly. He bore the burden to Calvary and suffered and died alone. Even two of Jesus' disciples desire leadership roles in His kingdom. They wanted a crown without the cross, a throne without the altar of sacrifice, and all the glory without the suffering that leads to it. Doesn't that sound like us today? We all want to share Jesus' glory but none of His suffering. Instead, we want to run and hide and cry because someone hurt our feelings. We want to pout and get an attitude because things didn't go our way. We want to slam doors and put people in choke holds all because they said something about us that we didn't agree with.

It is important for us to share His glory as well as His suffering because we must pick up our cross and follow after Him. Just like He was criticized, we would be criticized. In fact, I have been criticized for writing (long emails) and even had a former co-worker tell me that my little quotes (text messages) were becoming insults to him because he reads his Bible and have devotion every day. What my critics do not understand is that I do not sacrifice my time to glorify myself. I do it to glorify God. I am (we all are) ministers...servants, sent here to glorify God in all we do. Jesus could have stayed in heaven and watched us suffer alone. Instead, He left His home in heaven to come down to earth to die for our sins. Moreover, before He was spit on, denied, beaten, whipped, talked about, made fun of and criticized and eventually, deserted; He taught us how to live for God in spite of our present circumstances. He taught how to turn the other cheek when we are criticized for doing His Will. He taught us that to suffer for Him would bring more glory to Him as well as bring glory to ourselves. So why complain when people put you down for being a 'goody too shoes?' Why give up and walk away from God just because your wife/husband left you without a penny to your name? If you husband or wife left you, then he/she weren't meant to be with you anyway. Amen? Yes, we will make mistakes along the way and yes, we will come up against the raging seas of life, but we must dig our heels into the ground and hold on to God's unchanging hand.

The Holy Spirit helps us in our weakness. We must ask the Holy Spirit to intercede for us. One thing we need to understand is that once we become Christians, we gain all the privileges and responsibilities of a child in God's family. The Holy Spirit is one of the leading privileges. We may not always feel as though we belong to

God, but the Holy Spirit is our witness. His inward presence reminds of us who we are and encourages us with God's love. Moreover, just as we gain that outstanding privilege, we gain His suffering. So don't always expect smooth sailing in our walk with God. In fact, gear up with the whole armor of God. Be of good courage and be of good cheer. The battle is already won!

The God That Is In Me

"In whom ye also trusted, after that ye heard the word of truth, the gospel of your salvation: in whom also after ye believed, ye were sealed with Holy Spirit of promise." Ephesians 1:13 KJV

Ever wondered *what if?* What if I had taken the bus that day instead of a cab, I would have never met my husband/wife? On the other hand, what if my car had not broken down on the freeway; I could have been one of the many who lost their lives in that freak accident further down the road? What if I had decided to stop for coffee but did not so I was not there when the coffee shop was robbed and every poor soul that was in there was killed? I know, I know I made my point, but you must admit that it was pretty, eerie, right? It's the simple fact that one small thing could change the whole course of your life and you cannot help but to ask, what if?

I watched this movie called "Sliding Door." It was a decent movie. I liked it because the movie gave viewers a chance to see two different outcomes of the main character in the movie; what if this woman would have caught the train versus her missing the train.

I have heard within the contents of a prayer that an intercessor had prayed, "It is not I who do these things, but the God that is in me." That prayer touched me to the core of my heart. People are so quick to point out others' blemishes, weaknesses, and failings. Nevertheless, I dare them to point out others' strengths, potentials, and beauty. I dare them to allow others to see the God that is in them.

Think about how God ordained each of us for His glory. He divinely appointed us to take the cab instead of the bus, to miss that freak accident down the road due to our car trouble or missed a cup of coffee that spared us our life. God knew before you were born what your destiny would be. God has you right where He wants you to be. It may not be where you think you should be, but you are right where God wants you to be.

I want you to think about your divine appointments with God. This life, which you have claimed as your own, does not belong to you. You are not here for self, but to glorify Him. You are here to love God with all of your heart, your soul, and your mind with all of your might. You are here to love your neighbor as you love yourself. You must treat them the way you want to be treated. So stop talking about folks, stop trying to make yourself look better, and stop trying to hinder the gospel of Jesus Christ. And yes, you are hindering the gospel of Jesus Christ when you are knocking down His people instead of building them up. Moreover, you do not have to be on any executive board to feel important. Glory! Nor do you have to be in the front line of anything. Be more like Christ and consider yourself a lowly servant working diligently in the vineyard and being watchful in all you do for the Lord and for His people.

Be prayerful and remain watchful. The next time some gossip comes your way, delete it. The next time an opportunity comes your way to lift up someone's spirit, take that divine appointment with God to build up His spiritual kingdom. The next time you want to be seen in the limelight or receive credit for a job well done, give God the glory because had it not been for the God that is in you, you would not have been able to lift your head toward heaven.

Opening the Eyes of Your Heart

And Elisha prayed, and said, Lord, I pray thee, open his eyes, that he may see. And the Lord opened the eyes of the young man; and he saw: and, behold, the mountain was full of horses and chariots of fire round about Elisha. 2 Kings 6:17 KJV

I praise God for everything. I praise Him for my good days and for my bad days. I praise God for my late laying down and for my early rising. I praise God for my job, my health, my family and my loved ones and friends. I praise God for both the difficult situations and the difficult people I find myself facing from time to time. I praise Him especially during those difficult moments because it is under His wings, under His pavilion, and even in His shadows where I hide.

I am able to praise while dealing with difficult people because He opened the eyes of my heart. Once the eyes of my heart were opened, I was able to see things more clearly. I no longer looked at the world or the people of the world through my natural eyes but in the way that God sees them. See, I remember how patient God was with me when I was out in the world allowing the devil to use me. I remember how many times I wanted to sleep in on Sundays instead of going to church telling myself that it was the only day I could sleep in. I remember the number of times I made it to church, yet while I was there I kept looking at my watch counting down the minutes until service would be over. I remember how many times I woke up and went about my way without any harm or danger touching me or how may close calls I've had that could have ended badly, but didn't. Also, I remember how many times I was able to pay my bills when it seemed impossible.

But once my eyes were opened, nothing was impossible anymore. I looked to God for everything. Even dealing with difficult situations and/or people wasn't so bad either because I knew that God was in control over everything and He is still in control. I remember a conversation I had with a co-worker once about the 'haters' in our lives. I explained to her that haters are so afraid of us outshining them that they would do whatever it takes to deter us from shining. But they just don't know who they are up against. See, what haters fail to realize is that when we walk in God's anointing, man cannot touch us. Man cannot deter us from what God has already planned in our lives. What God has for us is for us. The fact is: once we allow the eyes of our hearts to be opened, we are completely submitting to God's Will. We will no longer look at people or situations the same way. Instead, we will see things and people as God sees them, like awaiting clay for the Potter's touch. Amen.

Thirsty for God's Living Water

For I will pour water upon him that is thirsty, and floods upon the dry ground: I will pour my spirit upon thy seed, and my blessing upon thine offsring. Isaiah 44:3 KJV

There is a need for God's living water. I see it in my own home, in schools, in grocery stores, on street corners, and in neighboring subdivisions. Everywhere I look, I see a need for His living water.

Sometimes our souls can become overwhelmed with day to day stuff leaving us dry and parched. Praying may even become a heavy task for us because of how burdened down we may feel. Sometimes, hopelessness will find its way into our minds and hearts and no matter what we do, relief may appear to be no where in sight. How do we approach the living waters of God to experience healing? The answer is to come in Jesus' Name and ask for what we seek. We keep praying. We PUSH forward meaning we will Pray Until Something Happens. We keep asking, seeking, and trusting in the God who open doors man cannot shut and trusting in the God who shut doors man cannot open. God will open our eyes to see beyond what's visible, truth beyond what's discernible, and life beyond our wildest imagination.

We all need God's living water so that we may have every need supplied, every want met, and every desire granted. We need to keep our focus on having a right relationship with God because without the relationship with Him, we will have no purpose, and without purpose, there would be no direction, and without direction, what would be the purpose for living? Think of areas in your life that need healing, growth, or that lack fruitfulness. Write these down as a list of prayer needs. When you use this list to pray, ask for God's living waters to bring this kind of help and relief. I'm encouraging you to pray daily, to go to God with gratitude and readiness to drink from His Word, and receive what you need from His Spirit and have your thirst quenched by His very presence with you.

Striving to the End

Strive to enter in at the strait gate; for many, I say unto you, will seek to enter in, and shall not be able. Luke 13:24 KJV

Do you understand why the Apostle Paul had so much zeal in his service to God? Do you understand why he willingly made his life a sacrificial offering to God each and every day after his conversion? Do you think he had a choice? Personally, I believe Paul didn't have a choice and neither do I. A fellow minister once asked me a question about the calling to preach the gospel. He asked me if any of us who were called to preach and teach the gospel had the choice to accept or decline the calling, would we?

Honestly, would you want to live a life that is not your own, putting aside your fleshly desires, personal accolades, and whatever else you may feel you want to do with your life? Could you imagine waking up each morning with a long to do list from God? Could you imagine preparing a sermon every week all the while having to deal with your own household issues, work issues, and children's issues, and having the responsibility of being made available to those who need prayer, to those who need encouraging, and even visit those who are in the hospital or home bound? Could you imagine the burdens one bear once called into the ministry? Ask yourself, how anyone could willingly give themselves over to God like that when we have choices. True, God gave us a free will but look at how our lives were before Christ. No joy, no peace, and no love. No quenching of the thirst and no satisfaction from that hunger. It was just us against the world.

The bottom line is this: Why fool yourselves into thinking that the world is a big playground and you can play in it as long as you want to when really; God has already measured the number of breaths we take. Why shorten our life spans by giving in to the temptation that if it feels good and looks good, then it must be good for us? Free will is God's way of allowing us to do what is right without twisting our arms to do it. Once our eyes are spiritually opened, it is our love for God and all that He has done for us that enables us to strive to the end. We wouldn't even question what God asked us to do, but willingly rise to the occasion and do whatever it takes to get the job done.

I read a quote from Billy Graham stating, "God proved His love on the cross. When Jesus hung, bled and died, it was God saying to the world—I love you." The Bible doesn't say what was going on in Jesus' mind as He hung on the cross, but His motivation for dying was He loved us and He was willing to do whatever it took to win our salvation. Strive to the end. Do whatever it takes to have life and have life more abundantly.

Haters

Do not I hate them, O Lord, that hate thee? And am not I grieved with those that rise up against thee? Psalm 139:21 KJV

We all have haters. A hater is someone who is jealous and envious of you and spends all of his/her time trying to make you look small or feel incompetent. Haters are negative people and nothing is ever good enough for them.

That's why we must be careful who we share our blessings with. Whatever success or blessings we are showered with; there will be those people who are going to try to minimize what it is we are doing. There will be some kind of controversial about how we went about doing something and the biggest problem is that haters cannot stand to see our glory. They cannot stand to see us have a beautiful relationship with God. They cannot stand to see how gifted or talented we are and how we are sharing our talents and gifts with others.

It's obvious who our haters are; just look for those who are always smiling too hard in our faces and they will be the first ones to tell us something that we are doing will not work. We must cut them off asking them do they know who our God is and what He is capable of doing? If that doesn't shut them up, try this: 'Watch me and my God work." They will really get ugly then because haters do not want to see us happy. They do not want to see us succeed nor do they want to see us get the victory.

So, for our haters, pray for them. As long as we know what our purpose is in life and doing what God ordained us to do, don't worry about them and allow God deal with them. Also, keep in mind, that whatever Satan uses to deter us, God will use it to bless and exalt us. Keep the faith. What we have is by divine prerogative and not human manipulation.

Those of us who are still trying to find that purpose in our lives, I want you to understand that purpose does not mean having a job. You can have a job and still be unfulfilled. A purpose is a clear sense of what God called you to be and is not defined by what others think about you. Keep living. Keep laughing. Keep praying.

His Amazing Grace

And they were all amazed at the mighty power of God. Luke 9:43 KJV

God's amazing grace is just that, amazing. I cannot put into words all that the Lord has done for me. We all have a beautiful testimony about what specifically He has done that led to our conversion. God's amazing grace can never fall short. He is an on-time God. He's majestic!!!! I've shared with my spiritual mentor/counselor about my increased awareness of God's glory. There are a lot of things that God has revealed to me. But that comes from spending a lot of quality and quiet time with Him in prayer and meditation. I often wondered when Jesus went into the mountains to spend some intimate time with His Father, what they talked about and if God answered Him audibly or quietly like He does with us.

There are no words for what I feel when I have scriptural moments such as Mark 1:35 or Luke 7 (the story about the centurion). At times, the sensation would be so overpowering that it would bring tears to eyes. And it's only because of His amazing grace and mercy that we are able to wake up every day in our right minds. It is because of His amazing grace and mercy that we are able to eat and clothes ourselves because He is our provider. It is because of His amazing grace and mercy that we are able to function on our daily vocations effectively. It is because of His amazing grace and mercy that we are no longer dead in our sins. And it is because of His amazing grace and mercy that we can open our mouths and praise Him…and if you know Him like I know Him, then His praises shall continually be in your mouth.

Remember that we serve a God that does not know how to fail so please do not give up on Him. How can you give up on the One True Living God who did not give up on you? Remain faithful to Him. Live each day glorifying God in all you do. It is not about you, but all about Him!

The Tree of Life

*In the midst of the street of it, and on either side of the river, was there
the tree of life, which bare twelve manner of fruits, and yielded her fruit
every month; and the leaves of the tree were for the healing of the nations.*
Revelation 22:2 KJV

I had a conversation with God once about ministering to the lost souls, the sick, and to those whose wounds have not been properly healed. I asked Him, how do you start the process of healing? How do you get to the bottom of the source that caused you pain that seeped so far down into your spirit that it festered until it hardened? How would you begin that process of healing? How is one able to use those stumbling blocks of the past and make them into stepping stones of the future? What if the very source that drained you is still draining you today? And how would you go about the process of healing if that source is a person and not a situation?

I do not walk around with my head too high thinking that I am above everyone else. Nor do I make a habit of frowning on people who haven't tapped into the One True Source of Life. I've even been accused of 'blocking things out' as a way of dealing with certain issues and relationships in my life. But is this true? Have I blocked out the bad things of the past so that I may deal with the present? How am I able to walk this walk with God and deal with the situations and issues that engulfs me? Before I can even minister to the lost souls, the sick and to those who have been wounded, I had

Undergo the healing process myself. I had to fall down on my knees and cry unto the Lord for help and I did not get up until I hear from Him. The flow of tears continued until His scarred Hand reached down to dry my weeping eyes. I asked God, "How can I teach someone to lean and depend on You? How can I assist people in the healing process? What can I say to make people understand that though it is hard, they must be willing to let it all go?" God whispered, "Show them." But isn't that what the Bible is for? I asked myself and a conversation with a fellow minister came to mind. It was during Sunday school and one of the students commented on how she wasn't being fed at church. I told her that she must feed herself and the minister asked, "what if she doesn't know how to?" Honestly, that question stumped me. As I looked around in my church, I could see hunger in the eyes of God's people. I could see their burning desire to have an intimate relationship with God and my next question is, "Are God's people being fed properly?"

I was led to Revelation 22, "*And He showed me a pure river of water of life, clear as crystal, proceeding out of the throne of God and of all the Lamb. In the midst of the street of it, on either side of the river, was there the tree of life which bare twelve manner of fruits…and the leaves of the tree were for the healing of the nations.* In order for any of us to be fed properly, we must be willing to take our eyes off our current or past situations or whatever it is that is causing us so much hurt and pain because in a nutshell, we cannot properly heal if we allow our situations to control us, our emotions, or the decisions we make. And whatever the situation is, it will not allow us to grow nor will it not allow us to feed ourselves. Moreover, it will give us a false sense of security when we try to block it out. Also, drugs and alcohol will not help us deal with our problems nor should we seek ungodly counsel.

In order for God to show you this pure river of water of life, you must be ready to see it through His eyes. You will not be able to see the many blessings that God has to offer if you are too busy looking at your situation. The tree of life is in my line of vision because I refused to allow sin to eat away at my blessings that God so freely gives. I refused to allow people to tear me down when God has already exalted me. (Did He not say, 'touch not thy anointed one'?) So please, refuse to allow your situations: past, present, or future to have control over you when the God we serve offers us rest for our souls.

Are You Really Who You Say You Are?

But above all things, my brethren, swear not, neither by heaven, neither by the earth, neither by any other oath: but let your yea be yea: and your nay, nay; lest ye fall into condemnation." James 5:15 KJV

The subject for one of my pastor's sermons was, 'Never Forget Who You Are.' He preached from Philippians 1:27-28. I took good notes because a lot of what he said rang true for many of us. Especially the part about how differently we act when we are away from 'church folk.'

I know that there are a lot of fake Christians in our churches. They are the ones who are very active in most of the organizations at our churches but if you asked them for one red penny, they'll guffawed at you muttering under their breath that they have paid their tithes and offerings. Then there are those who are 'saved, sanctified, and highly favored,' but they would not lift a finger to help anyone or do anything in the church. You all know who I am talking about, they are the ones who try to sit as close to the pulpit as possible, do most of the shouting, and quote scriptures from memory. Then of course, you have the ones who are genuine Christians, the faithful few who give until it hurts, pray more for others than they do for themselves, and give the best of themselves each and every time.

My question to you is this: which group do you belong in? Which of you, are really who you say you are? Don't you think it's embarrassing to be an ambassador of God when you're quick to cuss out someone for cutting you off in the street? Do you really think it's justice to call yourself a Christian, when you are one of many who keep liquor stores in business? (And no, I am not knocking drinking, but let's be honest with ourselves, a six pack or more in one night or one week is a bit much.) And for those of us who looked down on others because we feel that many do not 'dress up' enough, do you really think that God cares about how we dress on the outside as opposed to who we really are on the inside? I'm not even knocking those of us who step out in fresh gear on Sunday mornings. If you got it like that, by all means, do your thing, but also make sure that over that double-breasted suit or three piece skirt suit with the matching shoes, hat, and purse; you put on the whole armor of God because that is the only covering that will protect you from the enemy.

As I've stated in the many Sunday school classes: young adult and teenage girls, in many of my sermons/notes/letters; evaluate yourself on a regular basis. Check yourself before you try to check someone else. Stop getting on the phone every Sunday after church and run down people for the things that they have said, for what they had on, and even how they behaved in church. Honestly, what we should be discussing is the message that went forth and how we are going to internalize it for the week. We should be discussing what more could we do for those who are in need in the church and in our neighborhoods.

Be genuine in what you do and what you say. Stop spreading gossip and spread the Word instead. Do you really think you are going to heaven if all you are doing is tearing down God's people? Do you really think God is pleased with you if all you do is complain about what the church do and don't do? Ask yourself, am I really who I say I am? How do I act whenever I am not around my church family and would my behavior be pleasing to God? Don't expect changes to happen overnight and don't give up and walk away, if you find yourself making a lot of mistakes. All have sinned and fall short of glory of God. So don't give up but continue to strive in the Lord. Continue to be of good courage. Be steadfast in the faith and in the Word. Remember to love, encourage, and pray for one another.

Jesus is the Way, the Truth, and the Life

Jesus said unto him (Thomas), I am the way, the truth, and the life; no man cometh unto the Father, but by me. John 14:6 KJV

Jesus is the Way, the Truth, and the Life. How profound is that statement? What does it mean to us? Do we think about why Jesus told His disciple that while we are going through our trials and tribulations? Do we take the time to really meditate on what Jesus meant when He said, "I am the Way, the Truth, and the Life?"

There was nothing spectacular about my own conversion experience. I wasn't on the road going anywhere. I wasn't sitting on the rooftop in a daze. And I wasn't preparing to go fishing either. I was hurting and my heart was heavy and I remembered whispered, "*Jesus*," a five letter word that carries more weight and power than any electric company or power plant. I knew about Jesus, but I didn't know Him.

We all have read and studied about doubting Thomas. He was the disciple who had to see everything for him self in order to believe it. Are we like Thomas? Do we have to see miracles performed in order to believe that Jesus is still alive? Do we have to pray a prayer and have it answered immediately to know for sure that God is real? And what about our churches; are we waiting until we get there to ask for healing and prayers or do we put our faith in God and fall on our knees in supplication?

Twelve men walked and talked with Jesus, witnessing the Son of Man performing miracle after miracle, yet they still didn't know the extent of His power. They were still in awe of His awesomeness. One day, after calming the raging sea, Jesus turned to His disciples and asked, "*Where is your faith?*" My question to you today is, "Where is **your** faith?" When the sea of life is raging, are you focusing on Jesus being the Way; the pathway to heaven? So often, we hear that Jesus is a Way Maker, a Way of no way, but are we taking those facts to heart or are we repeating what we have heard? When the gas bill is high and the threat of eviction is weighing heavily on our shoulders, are we looking toward Jesus as the Truth, that He is who He says He is and He will do what He said He will do and His promise to never leave us nor forsake us is a guarantee? What about when our relationships take a toll on us and drain us spiritually? Do we seek Jesus' face and know that regardless of our family and friends forsaking us, He is always there to pick us up and carry us when we cannot do so on our own? Do we understand that we have life in Jesus and He is all that matters? Do we understand that putting Jesus first in all we do, we cannot fail at anything?

Back to my conversion experience: When I whispered, "Jesus," I was headed toward healing. In small faith, I took a step toward Someone who could help lead the Way. To Him, it did not matter if I knew how to pray or if I haven't been following Him all of my life. What mattered to Him was that I knew He could heal me. He knew I was tired of living a life of lies and I wanted to be genuinely happy. I wanted to have joy in my heart that no man, woman or child could ever take away from me. He knew that I sensed Him as the being the Truth that I had been looking for all of my life. And He knew that I wanted life and I wanted life more abundantly.

While you are at your desk, standing in line for lunch, or preparing yourself for prayer, I want you to ask yourself, "Where is my faith?" Do I put it in man or in God? Do I use my mouth to spread gossip or the gospel? How do I speak to those I love? How do I speak to those who I try to like but can't seem to? One more thing I want you to ask yourself, "Am I living to please God or am I living to please self? All of these questions will definitely keep you humble. Amen.

To Be Touched By God

And I will bring the blind by a way that they knew not: I will lead them in paths that they have not known; I will make darkness light before them, and crooked ways straight. These things will I do unto them, and not forsake them. Isaiah 42:16 KJV

"My Grace is sufficient for thee," He whispers. It is amazing how God speaks to me. He's so quiet. He always finds me whether I am standing in the midst of His beautiful creation surrounded by a pillar of trees or when I am staring up in a starry studded sky seeking Him. Oh how I yearned to be touched by God, for His spirit to breathe on me. It is simply beautiful how peace and serenity overcomes me when He finds me. *"I am always here,"* He reminds me. Like He has to, but I too, grow weak and weary and there is nothing wrong with needing to be restored from time to time.

I often imagined myself walking alongside the tranquil waters feeling a cool breeze caress me as it passes by. Though there are no other footprints on my walk, I know I am not alone. I do not even have to look over my shoulder out of fear because I am within His hedge of protection and there is neither danger nor any one that can cause or do harm to me.

There are times in my life when I cannot seem to get to the tranquil waters. Instead, I am positioned in front of a mountainous obstacle that is too high to climb or too wide to go around it. These are my trying times and instead of turning around to find my own way, I allow God to find a way for me. He leads me through these mountainous obstacles all the while holding onto my hand. *"Don't worry,"* He whispers. *"I am here with you always."* Once again, I am back by the tranquil waters.

Our forecast should always be "God reigns and His Son shines…" People often times try to find their own way in the sea of life and when they get to where the water is way over their heads, they cry out for a Life Savior. For some of them, it is too late while for others, He is an on-time God.

God anoints us, giving each of us a gift to share with the church, the community, or our families. A gift (or blessing) is a beautiful thing to have. It could be a smile, a hug, a touch on the shoulder, or a kind word. Sometimes, it could even be a message from God Himself. I do know that He speaks to me and through me but I have to be still in order to hear Him. Sometimes when I do hear Him, it moves me to tears because He loved me enough to show me His grace and mercy. But why me, what have I done to deserve His unconditional love when all I have said to Him was four little words? Yet, He saw fit to heal me, to prick my heart, to take the blinders from over my eyes. My walk has changed. My heart has been fixed and my mind, He regulated.

To be touched by God is a powerful, renewing experience and I am honored to share this poignant story with you. We all must continue to keep the faith and be of good courage. Sometimes in life, we have to be persistent like Jacob. We have to hold on to God until we receive a blessing. We must remember that when we are faced against opposition, we must allow God to take our hand and lead us through. Just as he always tell me and He has told you too, *"I am here with you always."*

The Devil Is a Liar

Ye are of your father the devil and the lusts of your father ye will do. He was a murderer from the beginning, and abode not in the truth, because there is no truth in him. When he speaketh a lie, he speaketh of his own; for he is a liar, and the father of it. John 8:44 KJV

You know, once we come to terms with what our purpose is in life, everything looks clearer, smell better, and our faith is strengthened. Whether we know it or not, knowing our purpose gives meaning to our lives. When life has meaning, we can bear almost anything, without it (purpose), nothing is bearable. Without God, life has no purpose and without purpose, life has no meaning. Without meaning, life has no significance or hope.

Knowing our purpose simplifies life. It defines what we do and what we don't do. Our purpose becomes the standard we use to evaluate which activities are essential and which aren't. Ask yourself, "Does this activity help me fulfill one of God's purposes for my life?" I promise you once you understand what your purpose is, you are better able to focus on your life as well as be motivated about that purpose. Being motivated promotes passion. We must understand that we weren't put on earth to be remembered, we were put on earth to prepare for eternity.

As for the devil being a liar, we should know by know that the devil has a way of coming into our thoughts, making us doubt why God created us in the first place. He has a way of using the people closest to us to tear us down and to try to break our spirit. He comes to steal, kill, and destroy. And he knows where our weaknesses are… he knows exactly when to come in and attack us. That's why God gave us a purpose and nothing is more important than knowing what that purpose is.

See, when we learn how to live a purpose-driven life, a life guided, controlled and directed by God's purposes, the devil has no place to rule in our minds, in our hearts, and in our lives. When he does come, we are already prepared. Think about it this way, when Jesus was in the wilderness, the devil attacked Him relentlessly. Knowing that Jesus had been without food or water for forty days, the devil used Jesus' weakness against Him. He told Jesus that He could easily turn the stone into bread and eat it and Jesus replied that man could not live by bread alone but by the Word of God. What we must strive to do is to find out what our purpose is (especially if we don't already know) and stick by it. Jesus couldn't be tempted in the wilderness because He knew what His purpose was in life. It wasn't about eating to sustain a physical need, it wasn't about tempting God nor was it about having all of the power without any of its suffering, but about living a purpose-driven life. It was about laying down His life for His sheep. With purpose in our hearts, in our minds, and in our daily lives, we'll be better able to see the devil for what he really is…a liar. God created us for more than just to accumulate worldly riches and accolades and the sooner we find out what our purpose is ….the better prepared we would be for eternity. Amen.

Our Maker

O Lord, *thou hast searched me, and known me.* Psalm 139:1 KJV

I remember telling my 'first friend' about how I could care less about what people said about me or even how they felt about me. Why should I care what people think about me when it was God who created me? In Psalm 139:13-14, the psalmist shared how he praised God for making such a wonderfully complex body...even doctors are amazed at how our bodies work. God is indeed a Masterful Creator!

God created me, breathing lie into my nostrils so why should I care if people do not like certain things about me? After all, God know everything about me, even to the number of hairs on my head. Whether people don't like the way that I talk or act or whatever it is; God still loves and accepts me for who I am. He is with me through every trial and tribulation---protecting me, loving me, and guiding me. Honestly, that's more than I say about those so-called friends who are always smiling in my face but talking about me behind my back.

Though I am not perfect, I am a work in progress. Just like God isn't finish with me, He is finish with you either. That's why James wanted the Christians in the church to pray for one another, because he knew the danger of false teaching as well as the danger of wolves coming in for the sheep. Just because a minister has a calling different from that of a Sunday school teacher, doesn't mean he/she doesn't need prayer. We are all intricate parts of the body of Christ. We have one God, one faith, and one driven purpose here on earth. We do not know what tricks Satan may have for us today, but we know prayer, and that's one of the main reasons why we must pray every morning before the start of our day.

Giving God all the praise, all the honor, and all the glory should not begin and end on Sunday mornings during worship services, but it should be a daily ritual; a way of life for the believer. I once asked God, how can I be a more effective witness to people I do not know? A few days later, someone sent me an email telling me how she forward my email to others. Some time before that, a good friend of mine revealed to me that he does the same thing to a friend of his with the text messages I send him every morning. Isn't God good? And I do not receive nor do I accept any glory, because it is not mine to have.

We must look to our Maker for directions in our lives and to show us our shortcomings and to ask for the strength and power to reverse our shortcomings into acts of up comings. Amen? When we live above reproach, no weapons formed against us shall prosper. May God's grace and mercy light your path of everlasting path. Be of good courage and continue to be faithful in His Word. Don't just read the Scriptures; let them soak deep into your spirit so that it will overflow into the lives of those you come into contact with.

Nothing is Too Big for Our God

Blessed are the undefiled in the way, who walk in the way of the Lord.
Psalm119:1

Hope. Faith. Endurance. Long-suffering. Peace. Mercy. Love. Patience. Self-control. I can go on and on describing the qualities of godly people. Could you imagine if more than one true Christian was in the Senate, on the board of education, in our schools, or driving our school buses? Could you imagine true Christians in their homes across the world raising children bearing before these children the foundation which Christianity is based on and what our world was created for?

Another historical moment surpassed us. One many of us never dared to dream or hope for. I could really care less the color of any candidate running for any office is…what matters to me most is this: Do they believe in the gospel of our Lord and Savior? Will they continue their quest in their purpose driven life once they are elected? Do they attend a faith-based, Bible teaching church? Would they be able to stand against the wiles of the devil or would they allow one tiny fraction of a problem deter them from their faith in God? Would they be able to stand for what is right and true and just even if they are the only one standing? Would they step out in faith before a large crowd of people not caring about offending anyone of another religion? All of these questions were racing through my mind as I prayed for our new president, President Barak Obama.

President Obama taking the stand to run for president two years ago gave America hope again. And I pray that throughout the next eight years (and yes, I said eight.) that President Obama would lead our country with the strength of God backing him to higher grounds. Let us continue to pray for our leaders of this great country. Though there are many of us who have never traveled outside the borders of USA, we are truly unaware of how good we have it in America. Our food, for the most part, is ok. We have access to clean drinking water, we have a voice that we can use, plus we have many rights and laws that protect us…whereas many of these third world countries have nothing to protect them or their rights.

In my closing, please continue to be prayerful about our country's leaders. Stop thinking that your vote or your voice does not matter. It does! Imagine that your voice is like a ripple in a pond. It starts off small but grows and spreads throughout the entire pond touching every in its path. That's the affect our voices have on our communities, our cities, and our states. One person can change the course of another person's life which that person could have the same affect on someone else and that cycle goes on and on. Another thing we must be doing is thinking small. Think bigger. God wants the best for each of us and in order for us to get the best we must think bigger and elevate our faith in Him. Won't He make a way of no way?

My Saving Grace

For ye know the grace of our Lord Jesus Christ, that, though he was rich, yet for your sakes he became poor, that ye through his poverty might be rich. 2 Corinthians 8:9 KJV

I have been active on the advisory committee of the Greater Fellowship Outreach Ministry and Development Services for four years as well as the assistant editor for the program's bi-monthly newsletter, "Visions of Hope." This outreach ministry hosts feeding programs that includes giving food baskets and/or clothes to the needy and homeless. Moreover, for the holidays, Thanksgiving and Christmas, they extend their services to Dekalb County Department of Family and Children Services where 10 or more families are given food, clothes, and toys. The ministry also hosts an annual health fair that is open to the church and the community at large. People from the community can get their blood pressure, glucose, and iron checked. This ministry is also committed to supplying school supplies and free weekly tutorials to those in need during school sessions.

Recently, we have been trying to tap into the prison ministry facet. As Christians, it is part of our missionary work to go into the fields to labor, not to sit around and watch others do it. I am passionate about this work because they are so many people who are without homes, without food, without proper clothing. In Matthew 25: 34-45, Jesus told His disciples to feed those who are hungry, to dress those who are naked, and to visit those who are in the hospitals and behind prison walls. Anything that I read and study concerning the Word of God, I take to heart. It pierces my heart and leads me to action. Isn't that part of Christianity; reading and studying the Word of God, applying those scriptures to your heart, and then set out to do His Will?

I am sure we all have busy and conflicting schedules that keep us from getting more involved with various church organizations. I teach Sunday School for the teenage girl's class, mentor, sing in the contemporary church choir, tutor, and I am active in the outreach ministry, not to mention what I do after school at my job with Dekalb County. The point that I am making is this: If God saw fit to wake you up in the morning, clothing you in your right mind, with the use of all your limbs, if God saw fit to feed you, clothe you, to see to it that you are healthy; that you have eye sight (to read and study the Word of God), that you have speech to witness to someone abut the power of God's perfect love. If God saw fit, just to be that Mountain Mover, to be that Bridge over troubled waters, that Prince of Peace, that Shield of Protection, that Bright and Morning Star, that Lily in the Valley, that Mind Regulator and Heart Fixer…if God saw fit to do all of those tings and much, much more, why is it so hard to make our lives a living altar for God? How can we continue to be so stingy with our time, our money, and ourselves?

Are you truly living for God in every facet of your life? Are you glorifying God by the work that you are doing? Are you witnessing to the people at your jobs, in the grocery stores, on the street corners, in your children's schools or daycares? Are you giving your time, your money and of yourself until it hurts? When you see that hungry man or woman, do you turn your nose up at them assuming that they are going to buy alcohol or drugs with your hard earned money? When you see a need in your own neighborhood, do you wait until somebody else make a move to handle it or do you take the initiative? These are questions that I ask myself as well. I evaluate myself everyday. I am pulling off the flesh and putting on the whole armor of God. That is a must!

I pray that this message edifies you, inspiring you to do much more than going to work and attending weekly Bible studies, and worship services. Keep God first in everything you do. He should be at the head of our lives and the sooner we realize that, the better off we will be. Of course, putting Him first will not rid us of drama-free lives, but God will give us the courage, the strength, and the peace to handle anything that tries to knock us off course.

On a more personal note, without the grace of God, I would have been in my grave a long time ago. I could have been peddling for food or money for my hungry children at home, or I could have been strung out on drugs selling my body to support my drug habit. By working in the different ministries inside and outside my church, those are the saving graces which enables me to strive in my continuance of fulfilling God's will. These saving graces enable me to identify and submit to what God's purpose is for my life. I pray that you will gain an understanding of how incredible our God is and how He deserves incredible praise. If God saw fit to save you from your sins, what are you going to do for Him in return?

It's Not What People Call You;
It's Who You Answer To

Therefore thus saith the Lord, if thou return, then will I bring thee again, and thou shalt stand before me: and if thou take forth the precious from the vile, thou shalt be as my mouth: let them return unto thee; but return not thou unto them. And I will make thee unto this people a fenced brazen wall: and they shall fight against thee, but they shall not prevail against thee: for I am with thee to save thee and to deliver thee, saith the Lord. And I will deliver thee out of the hand of the wicked, and I will redeem thee out of the hand of the terrible. Jeremiah 15: 19-21 KJV

Jesus asked His disciples, after hearing all the things that people referred to Him as, *"But who do you say I am?"* Some people thought that Jesus was one of the prophets who had risen from the grave or just a gifted teacher, but Peter boldly claimed Jesus to be the Christ, the Son of the living God.

In a message I preached at the Nursing Home, I shared with them how God had been dealing with me, I shared how I referred go those times as wilderness period because it is during those times when God is preparing me for the next level of His ministry. During this wilderness period, God placed in my spirit the weeping prophet Jeremiah. I shared how heavy the burden was that Jeremiah had to carry. Not only could he not get married, but he was abandoned by family, friends, and loved ones due to God's calling on his life. Meanwhile, Jeremiah had to preach to hard-headed people confronting them of their blatant sins and even his message to them was simple: 'Repent, turn to God, or He will punish.' Of course, no one wants his/her sins confronted and pointed out and as a result of that, there was a plot to kill Jeremiah. Could you imagine your life being threatened because of what God ordained you to do?

Although Jeremiah and Jesus were both talked about, despised, hated, plotted against, and even killed for carrying out God's Will;

they refused to allow what people called them to deter them from completing God's Will. But of course, Jesus was the only One who died for the sins of the entire world and rose again so that sinners wouldn't have to die in their transgressions. Amen?

My point is this: people will talk about you no matter what you say or do. No matter how obedient and faithful you are to God and His Word, people are going to call you out of your name, make assumptions about you, and degrade you in any way they can. But those are just the toppings on your sundae. It is not what people say about you, what people call you, or what they may do to you, but its how you answer, who you answer to, and how you respond to their mistreatment of you is what is important. It's also knowing that you know that you know that you know who your Father is in Heaven and what His purpose is for your life.

Jesus knew what His purpose was and He was determined to pick up that old rugged cross and carry it up that hill. Even though He had been whipped and beaten the night before, He withstood those nails going into His hands and feet. Although the pain was unbearable and Jesus was abandoned by His own men, He endured because He knew that in three days, He would rise again. He hung, bled, and died just so that we all would know the way to Heaven.

So, faithful servants of God, continue to rise above what ever the enemy set before you and look to the hills from whence cometh your help. God is our strength and fortress, a refuge in the day of trouble! He is our strength when we are weak, a fortress when our enemies attack us, and a refuge when we need rest. Amen!

Wounded in the Church

They shall put you out of the synagogues: yea, the time cometh, that whosoever killeth you will think that he doeth God service. And these things will they do unto you, because they have not known the Father, nor me. John 16:2-3 KJV

How many of us have been wounded in the church by someone who claimed to have the love of God in his/her heart but mistreated us as if we were beneath him/her? How many of us have been accused of doing something that we know we didn't do? How many of us have been neglected and abused by the very people who claimed that God put them in charge of us? How do we heal from such wounds? How do we move pass the pain and disappointment? How do we open our hearts to receive God's unconditional love when our hearts have been bruised and crushed? Honestly, it isn't easy moving pass any pain. It isn't easy forgiving those who hurt us beyond repair especially when those wounds are caused by someone of a leadership position. But how? How do we move on? How do we keep from allowing what one person has done to us to affect our willingness to trust others?

It may sound redundant but honestly it will take prayer and time to heal all wounds. You have to literally give it all over to God to work it out for you and I am a living witness to that. You cannot allow what one person has done to affect how you live your life for God. Don't allow a church to make you walk away from God. Don't allow your trials and tribulations (which will come to make you strong) to stop you from giving God your praises. You must rely on God's strength to lead you through those valleys of life. You must stand on His Word and remember that God is a Healer, a Mighty Stronghold, a Bridge over Troubled Water. You must remember that it is His Way, His path that you must walk on and as long as you are following Him, can't nothing break you, stop you or tear you down. Be strong in the Lord and in all His might. Be blessed. We must also remember that there is no such thing as a bad day. We are blessed the moment we wake up. We are blessed the moment we are able to get out of bed and dress and feed ourselves. We must remember who our Father is and that there is nothing impossible to those who believe in Him. Amen.

Into the Soul of a Christian Woman

From the inner part of Man,
God made a woman.
He is the Master Craftsman
who molded her with His skillful hands.
Divinely sculpturing her most delicate
treasures,
He whispers a secret into her ear
igniting vestibules of wisdom
engraving them into her spirit.
Before He saw that 'it was good,'
He intakes a sharp breath
and expels air
into her lungs
making her into a living soul.
The soul of a Christian woman
is more precious than rubies.
She is clothed with strength and dignity
and speaks from a heart of pure wisdom.
She is not only prayerful,
but watchful in all she says and does
making sure she lives above reproach.
For she also knows
that God's creative work
was not complete until He made
 her---
A Christian woman.

About the author

Satara P Ferguson is a gifted speaker, sensational writer, and uplifting Sunday School teacher. She is a Youth Minister at Greater Fellowship Missionary Baptist Church in Decatur, GA. She teaches Sunday school, Bible study, and conduct bi-monthly youth worship services and looks for opportunities to assist/minister to the needs of others. She is passionate about mentoring the youth and setting the pace in which they can soar.

Ferguson works for Dekalb County Schools as an interrelated teacher at an elementary school in Clarkston, GA. She is a member of Zeta Phi Beta Sorority, Inc. She is currently seeking her Masters in Christian Education at the Interdenominational Theological Center in Atlanta, Georgia.

She has published other poems, short stories, and is currently seeking a publisher for her Christian novel, **Leave Well Enough Alone** and its sequel, **All Is Well That Ends Well. Confessions of a Well-Kept Woman** is her second inspirational book.

She lives with her husband Chasoray Newton, Sr. and sons, HyKeem and Chasoray, Jr., and their dog Roxie in Lithonia, Georgia.

About the book

Confessions of a Well-Kept Woman is an empowering journey of soul stirring and uplifting inspirational pieces that expresses the author's conviction of her faith. Through out each page, she challenges readers to walk by faith and not by sight, fall head-over-heels in love with the Creator, and to grow spiritually and become more Christ-like every day.

Satara P. Ferguson admits that this is an expedition on a road less traveled by and there will be bumps, mountainous obstacles, and potholes along the way, but believes with all of her heart that it is well worth the journey.

Enter ye in at the strait gate: for wide is the gate, and broad is the way, that leadeth to destruction, and many there be which go in thereat: Because strait is the gate, and narrow is the way which leadeth unto life, and few there be that find it. Matthew 7:13-14 KJV

Acknowledgements

I want to give special thanks to Evangelist Sandra Parks and Evangelist Andrea Woodbine for agreeing to write the forewords for me. I am the one who is honored. Thank you for being true friends! You have truly inspired me to step out of my comfort zone and aspire for greatness.